Read to Me

by Sheila Smith

Illustrated by Angela Mills

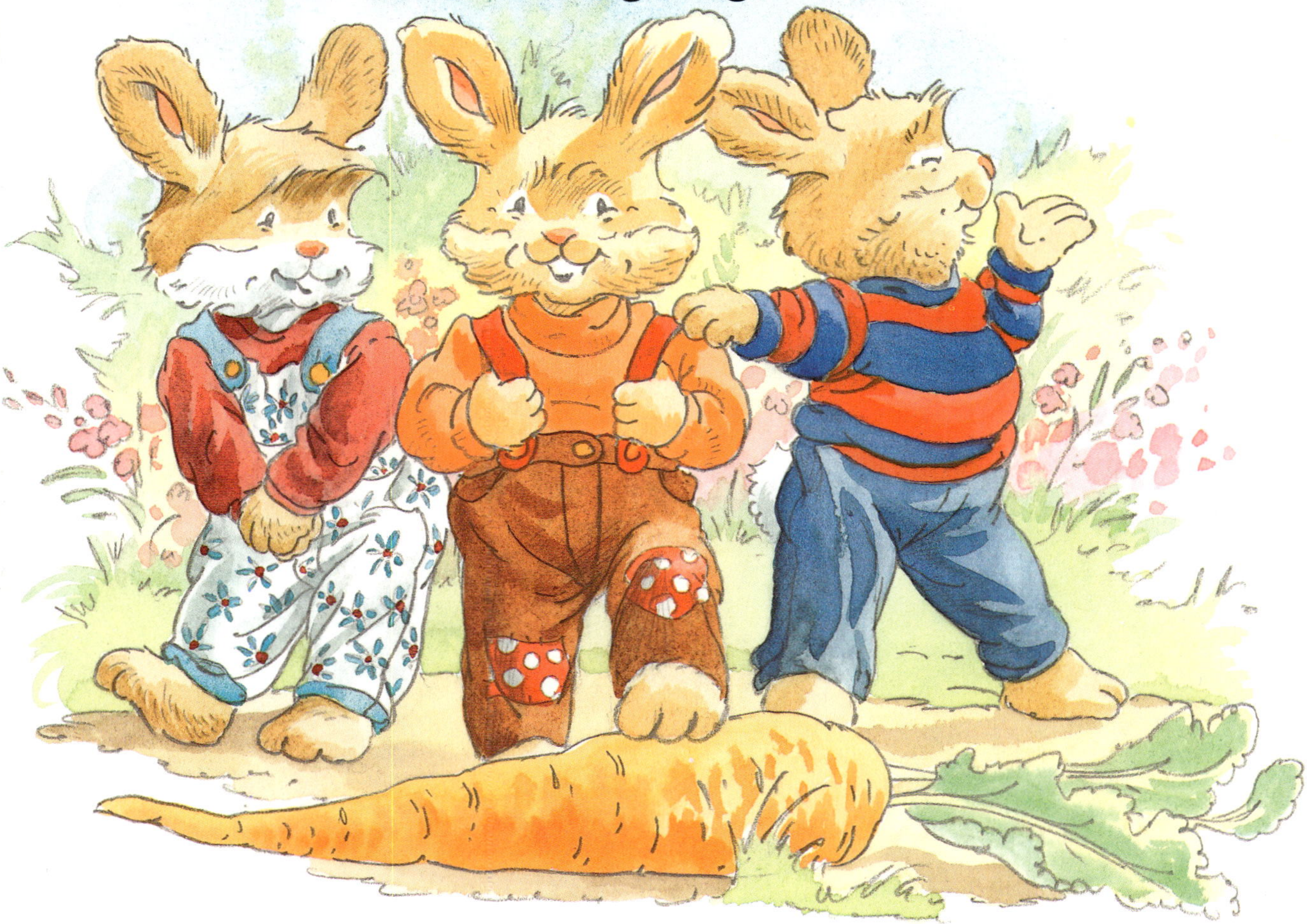

BRIMAX · NEWMARKET · ENGLAND

Mr and Mrs Rabbit are out in the garden.
Rags, Roly and Rosie are helping them.
"I wish I could have my own garden," says Rosie. "Then I could grow my own carrots!"
"I will help you," says Roly.
"And me!" says Rags.

Mr Rabbit laughs and says, "You can have a piece of this garden if you promise to look after it!"

"Oh, thank you!" say Rosie, Rags and Roly.

Mr Rabbit shows them the piece of garden they can have.

Rosie picks up a little shovel and starts to dig. Rags starts to pull out the weeds and Roly holds the bucket.
Soon their little garden is ready for some seeds.
"Please can we have some carrot seeds?" they ask their father.

Mr Rabbit gives them a packet of carrot seeds.
"Thank you!" they say.
Rosie digs the holes, Roly puts in the seeds and Rags waters them. They like gardening.
"I cannot wait for the carrots to grow," says Rags.

The very next day, the three little rabbits run outside to look for carrots. They are disappointed when they cannot see anything.

"It will take a little longer than that for your carrots to grow," laughs Mr Rabbit.

Every day either Rosie, Roly or Rags check to see if the carrots have started to grow. One day Roly gives a shout, "I have found some carrots! Look Rosie and Rags!" The two rabbits come running and sure enough, right in the middle of their little garden are some carrot stalks.

"Let's pull them out!" says Rags.
Rosie pulls all the carrots up but one will not move. Then Roly tries but he cannot move it either. The three rabbits all pull together and the biggest carrot ever comes out of the ground!

"Wow!" says Rags. "It's enormous!"
The three rabbits take the carrot to show their mother and father.
"Goodness me!" says Mrs Rabbit. "Did you grow that?"
"Yes!" says Rosie. "Does this mean we are good gardeners?"
"Very good ones!" laughs Mr Rabbit.

The three rabbits are very proud of themselves. They help their mother prepare the carrot for dinner. They are having carrot stew.
When they have eaten it they are all full. They all agree that Rosie, Roly and Rags grow the biggest carrots ever!